CREATIVE MEDITATIONS FOR CHILDREN

TAMING

Monster Moments

Turning On Soul Lights
to Help Children Handle Their Fear and Anger

By Daniel J. Porter

✦

Illustrations by Cheryl Nathan

Paulist Press
New York/ Mahwah, N.J.

For Barbara, Chelsey & Karoline.
— Love Always, D.J.P.

For Deborah Davey, for friendship and insight.
— C.N.

Cover design by Cheryl Nathan

Porter, Daniel J., 1961–
        Taming monster moments : turning on soul lights to help children handle their fear and anger / by Daniel J. Porter ; illustrated by Cheryl Nathan.
                p.   cm.
        Summary: Acknowledges times when we feel afraid or angry and suggests ways to focus on positive statements relative to such experiences.
        ISBN 0–8091–6655–0 (alk. paper)
        1. Fear in children—Juvenile literature. 2. Anger in children—Juvenile literature. 3. Anxiety in children—Juvenile literature. [1. Fear. 2. Anger. 3. Conduct of life.] I. Nathan, Cheryl, 1958– ill. II. Title.
BF723.F4P67 1999
155.4′1246—dc21
                                                                        98–30150
                                                                             CIP
                                                                              AC

Published by Paulist Press
997 Macarthur Boulevard
Mahwah, New Jersey 07430

www.paulistpress.com

Printed and bound in
Hong Hong

TAMING MONSTER MOMENTS

Turning On Soul Lights
to Help Children Handle Their Fear and Anger

Have you ever seen a monster? I have.

Monsters come in all shapes, sizes and colors.

Like the monsters we see on our favorite television shows. They make us laugh as we watch them snort, roar, run and jump.

There are monsters which appear on the pages of the books we read. Green, purple, orange, polka dots, stripes—you name it. When we close the book, we know these monsters stay inside. We're glad these are "just pretend."

And then there is another kind of monster: an invisible monster that appears inside us when we feel afraid. This monster really scares us because we don't know what to do when it sneaks inside a mean thought or an unhappy feeling. Sometimes that inside monster shouts at us—and maybe at other people, too.

Let me tell you about something I've learned. There is something wonderful we can do about this monster inside us. We can turn on the special light that lives deep inside us in our souls, to chase those monsters away. Just as we do in our houses at night.

This light inside us is so powerful, it never burns out or needs new batteries.

This special soul light is so strong, it shines through our spirits and helps us not to be afraid.

I wrote this book especially to show you how to take care of this monster by turning on your inside soul light. So, get ready to turn the page. Read the description of each "monster moment." Then ask yourself: "How would I feel with such a monster inside me? What would I *do* if this monster were inside me?"

Turn the page again. Read each **Turning On Your Soul Light** hint and find each helping tip, hidden in the illustrations, to help you turn on your inside soul light. And watch how you change from a roaring monster back into the real, terrific YOU.

Monster Moment:

"Nothing I ever do turns out right."

I hate it when this happens:
Sometimes when I talk, my words don't say what I was really feeling.
"You have a fat tummy," the unkind monster inside me says.
What I really meant to say was, "Your tummy is as soft as a pillow.
I like laying my head against you."
Sometimes when I make a picture, what I draw on paper
doesn't look like the picture I saw in my imagination.
"I'm going to throw away this ugly picture,"
the criticizing monster inside me says.
And sometimes when I try to help,
things don't turn out quite the way I wanted.
Cr-a-ash! The dishes I was trying to carry fell to the floor.
"I can't do anything right!" the unhappy monster inside me says.

Turning On Your Soul Light

"Trying your best is the best you can do."

No one can do things perfectly every time.
Hardly anyone is good at something the first time he or she tries.
What matters most is that we try, and that we give our best.
We need to be patient with ourselves.
Then, if things don't turn out quite the way we'd like,
we know we can always try again.

Monster Moment:

"I don't want to play with you anymore!"

Why should I play a game
just because my brother or sister
or friend wants to?
"How come you always get to make
all the decisions?"
"It's not fair! We always do what
you want to do."
"You don't play right."
"I don't want to play with you anymore,"
the crabby monster inside me says.

**"The best way to forget what you don't like
is to remember what you do like."**

Sometimes brothers, sisters and friends make us angry.
Then we forget how happy they make us at other times.
Imagine anger as a big monster,
making us forget everything we like.
What can we do?
First, we need to help the monster calm down.
Then it's time to think about why
we like our brothers, sisters and friends.
Remembering what we like most about someone
is the best way to forget what we like least.

Monster Moment:

"I'm too little to help somebody else."

Today we passed some people on the street
who don't have a home.
It makes me feel sad to think of people
who have nowhere to come home to,
with no place to get warm when it's cold outside,
no place to sleep when it's time for bed,
no place to play inside when it's raining outdoors.
"I'm too little to help somebody else,"
the helpless monster inside me says.

"Opening our hearts often opens our eyes...and our hands."

When we open our hearts, it often opens
our eyes and our hands.
Now we see a way we can help someone
who needs us—no matter how old we are.
One person can't help everyone.
But, each of us has something special
to give to others. If we join with others,
our "little somethings" will add up
to make a BIG difference.

Monster Moment:

"Those kids aren't like me."

I see some kids at playgrounds,
at stores and places where we eat …
and they're not like me.
Sometimes they talk in words I don't understand.
Their clothes, the way they look,
the things they like to do are strange.
Sometimes I don't know what to do or what to say
when I am around others who aren't like me.
"He talks weird" or "she looks funny,"
the criticizing monster in me says.

Turning On Your Soul Light

"We're all the same...because we're all different!"

Isn't it wonderful that our world is filled with
flowers of different colors and smells,
birds that sing different songs,
animals of different shapes and sizes,
and people of different races.
Wouldn't it be boring if everything and
everyone were exactly the same?
The one thing all of us have in common is
that we're all different.
Remember: whenever you notice someone
who is different than you, that person is probably
noticing the same thing about you.

Monster Moment:

"I always forget things I'm supposed to remember."

I always forget things I'm supposed to remember. I try to put my thoughts and words in a safe place in my mind. But, when I try to find them they're gone!

And sometimes I forget to put away my clothes, toys and other things.
Then, when I do put my things away, sometimes I can't remember where I put them.
That's when I get frustrated and even angry.
"I can't ever find anything!" the upset monster inside me says.
Or, "Somebody must have taken my book!" the frustrated monster inside me blames.

"Bit by bit, you'll remember more and more."

Do you remember when you didn't know your ABC's,
or your colors, or the words to your favorite songs?
You learned all of those things because you
practiced them over and over.
To build a better memory, practice every day.
Bit by bit, you'll remember more and more.

Monster Moment:

"If I share, there will be less for me."

I love getting presents.
I love how they look when they're tucked under the branches
of a Christmas tree or stacked on a table waiting for a birthday
party to begin. I love the colors of the wrapping paper
and the loud sound it makes when you r-r-rip it off.
I love all the presents my family and friends have given me.
I want to keep them with me always.
I have to wait a long time to get my presents.
And then, as soon as I get them, someone asks me to share.
That's not fair!
"If I share, there will be less left for me,"
the selfish monster inside me says.

Turning On Your Soul Light

"When you give to others, you also give to yourself."

Isn't it fun to see the surprise on someone's face
when he or she pulls back the wrapping paper
of your gift to see what you put inside?
Try counting the many ways that you can give…
…like sharing your smile…
…like being kind when someone needs it most…
…like helping out someone when he or
she needs a helping hand.
Giving to others can be so much fun—
it's like giving yourself a present.

Monster Moment:

"I always have to stop doing what I like to do. Nothing fun ever lasts and that makes me mad!"

I love weekends!
They're so much fun!
I watch movies, eat treats,
and play with my friends.
It's great!
But, no matter how much fun weekends are,
they always end.
I really like ice cream!
I love how it tastes inside my mouth
and makes me shiver.
But, no matter how hard I try,
the ice cream never lasts very long.
It makes me angry when I have to stop doing
the things I like to do.
"No, I won't stop playing and
go to bed now,"
the stubborn monster inside me says.

Turning On Your Soul Light

"Life is full of beginnings and endings... endings and beginnings."

Look at a circle.
Can you tell where it begins?
Do you know where it ends?
Our lives—with all the fun we have, with all the love we give—
can be like circles that never end.
Instead of thinking only about what is ending,
think about what else is just beginning.
If you have to stop playing a game,
think about how much fun you'll have
the next time you play it; think about the fun
you'll have while doing something else.
Each new minute of each new day brings us
another chance to discover endings and beginnings,
beginnings and endings.

Monster Moment:

"I'm scared, but I can't tell anyone."

I get scared by lots of things—
pictures on television, shouting on my street,
kids fighting on the playground.
Sometimes when I am going to school
I can feel the monster inside me making me scared.
Then I'd rather stay at home.
I don't want to tell anyone because I want everyone
to think I'm big and brave—even though sometimes
I'm not. Sometimes, when I wake at night, I feel a little
frightened even though my night light is on and my family is
close by.
"I can't call for somebody because then everybody will know
I'm scared," the worried monster inside me says.

Turning On Your Soul Light

"Your soul light can shine through all the darkness."

The darkness that sits in our rooms at night can't hurt us. The darkness inside mean words and actions can't hurt us. We have our soul lights deep inside us that will shine through, and we can see by those lights that we have nothing to fear. Try not to feel bad when you feel afraid. Even saints, presidents and heroes felt scared sometimes, too. Being brave doesn't mean not feeling afraid. Being brave means remembering to turn on our soul lights inside us.

Monster Moment:

"I'm so mad, I'm never going to talk to you again!"

When someone is mean to me I tell myself I will never be nice to that person again. Sometimes it makes me feel better to feel angry.

Sometimes when I'm angry with someone who hurt or disappointed me, I want to stay mad for a long time.

"I'm so mad, I'm never going to talk to you again," the angry monster inside me says.

"We all make mistakes...we all deserve another chance."

Everyone makes mistakes sometimes.
When we become angry because of someone's mistake,
we need to take a few moments to think
before we say or do anything else.

Think of a time when you hurt someone else
because of something you said or did.
Remember how badly you felt,
knowing that someone was angry with you.

Now, try to remember how good it felt
when that person forgave you
and you became friends again.

It's your turn to make someone
else feel good by forgiving.

We all make mistakes...
we all deserve
another chance.

Monster Moment:

"No one is paying any attention to me!"

Everyone around me is too busy for me—
my parents, brothers and sisters, even my friends.
Sometimes they all have things they want to do
and no one wants to do anything with me.
Who is going to sing and laugh,
play games and ride bikes,
roller skate and paint and draw,
hike and hunt for fireflies with me?
"Nobody is paying any attention to me,"
the lonely monster inside me says.

"When someone can't play with you, ask to join someone else."

When everyone is too busy to do the things you want to do,
either find something you like to do alone,
or ask to join someone else's activity.
Joining someone else's work or play
is a very good way to keep from feeling lonely and left out.
Chances are, once you've spent time
working or playing with others,
they'll probably be ready to do what you like next.

Monster Moment:

"I don't feel very special."

When I look around and see millions of people in the world, who know how to do millions of special things, like building houses and making machines, like dancing and singing, drawing and writing, like taking care of children, or helping sick people, and many, many more—
I wonder: How can I be special? How can I do something new that no one else has ever done? Or do something better than anyone else?
I'm not the best at anything—not arts, crafts, music, sports or making people laugh. "I don't feel very special," the scared monster inside me says.

"You are one-of-a-kind."

Take another look around our huge world with the wonderful animals,
things in nature, and millions of people.
How many of those people look exactly like you?
How many of those people have your name, play with your toys
and your friends, live with your family and say "I love you" to
the people you love?
Of all those wonderful animals, things and people YOU are the
only person who can do things in your special way.
And that makes you…one-of-a-kind.

Monster Moment:

"I can't stop feeling sad."

Sometimes no matter how hard I try
I can't seem to stop
feeling sad.

Nothing seems to help.
Watching television
doesn't help.
Playing with my friends
doesn't help.

Not even holding my
favorite stuffed animal helps.
Some of me wants to
have fun, play and laugh,
but most of me is feeling
too sad.

"This sad feeling is never
going away,"
the crying monster
inside me says.

"Something good will grow from sadness."

Has it ever rained on a day
when you really wanted
to play outdoors?
When we're inside watching
raindrops hit the window,
wishing that we could be
playing outside,
it's hard to remember
that nature needs the rain
to help make things grow.
The trees we love to climb,
the grass in our parks and ball fields,
the carrots, lettuce and corn
in our gardens, the apples,
oranges and peaches in our
orchards and groves—
all need rain to make them grow.
Sadness is like rain.
When it comes,
we have to remember
that the rain will pass.
Something good will grow
from our sadness.

Monster Moment:

"I don't want to wait! I want it now!"

"Please wait your turn."
"You'll have to wait until tomorrow."
"You're still too little…wait until you're bigger."
"Now now—wait until your friends come."
"Just wait until I've finished doing this…"

"WAIT A MINUTE! I'M TIRED OF WAITING!"
the impatient monster inside me says.

Turning On Your Soul Light

**"Caterpillars become butterflies
only by waiting."**

Imagine how good it feels flying like a butterfly.
Flittering, fluttering, floating in the air—
it must feel great.

Now think about when that butterfly was just a caterpillar—
how hard it had to work
to crawl just a few inches on the ground.

When that caterpillar was tightly wrapped in its cocoon,
did it feel it would have to wait forever
before it could fly?

But…the right time always comes
for butterflies and people.

Whenever you feel like a caterpillar
who has to crawl so sl-o-w-ly,
imagine the time
when you'll be flying high.

Monster Moment:

"I'm afraid of the bullies at my school."

There are bullies at my school. They make me feel afraid.
I don't like it when they act mean and shout bad words at my
friends and me. Why does this happen?
As soon as they walk near us we feel afraid.
The words they say to us make us feel terrible.
Sometimes we do what they say because we hope they'll leave us alone.
It's not fair. And it's not fun. "Why doesn't somebody do something about
those mean old bullies?" the scared monster inside me says.

Turning On Your Soul Light

"Make the bullies disappear by doing nothing."

It's not easy to deal with bullies, especially when they make us feel that there is nothing we can do.
And nothing at all is the best thing to do to bullies.
Bullies like to see us become nervous and afraid.
They want us to shout back at them because then they can feel strong and powerful.
When we do nothing bullies don't know what to do.
When we do nothing it means their words and actions have not hurt us. Bullies are people who are asking for attention in a bad way.
Bullies can't be bullies if they have no one to bully.

Grump! groan! growl!

Snarling Monster Moments can appear
To make us hiss and howl
With feelings of anger or fear.
But now we know how we might
Chase those monsters away—
By turning on our soul lights
We shine in what we do and say.
Give your brother a special smile
And hold your sister's hand,
And if you sit with a friend awhile
You will understand
That, though there sure can be
Difficult days to live,
Life's better for you and me
Whenever we love and forgive.
Please read these pages like a guide
Over and over again
Whenever you have a monster inside
Who needs you as a Best Friend.

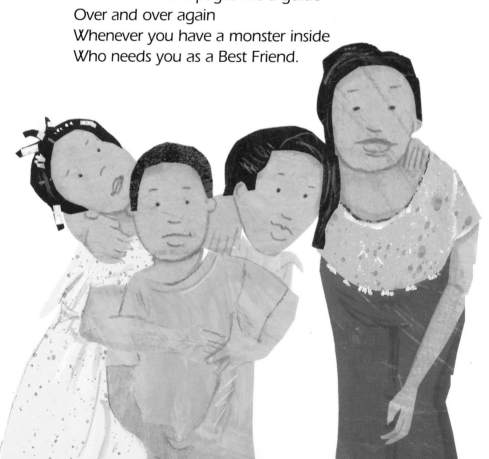